IT'S TIME TO BAKE GINGERSNAP COOKIES

It's Time to Bake GINGERSNAP COOKIES

Walter the Educator

Silent King Books
A WhichHead Entertainment Imprint

Copyright © 2025 by Walter the Educator

All rights reserved. No part of this book may be reproduced in any manner whatsoever without written per- mission except in the case of brief quotations embodied in critical articles and reviews.

First Printing, 2025

Disclaimer

This book is a literary work; the story is not about specific persons, locations, situations, and/or circumstances unless mentioned in a historical context. Any resemblance to real persons, locations, situations, and/or circumstances is coincidental. This book is for entertainment and informational purposes only. The author and publisher offer this information without warranties expressed or implied. No matter the grounds, neither the author nor the publisher will be accountable for any losses, injuries, or other damages caused by the reader's use of this book. The use of this book acknowledges an understanding and acceptance of this disclaimer.

It's Time to Bake GINGERSNAP COOKIES is a collectible early learning book by Walter the Educator suitable for all ages belonging to Walter the Educator's Time to Bake Book Series. Collect more books at WaltertheEducator.com

USE THE EXTRA SPACE TO TAKE NOTES AND DOCUMENT YOUR MEMORIES

GINGERSNAP COOKIES

It's time to bake, oh what a treat,

It's Time to Bake
Gingersnap Cookies

Gingersnap cookies, warm and sweet!

With sugar, spice, and lots of cheer,

A perfect snack when winter's near.

Gather the flour, soft and white,

Measure it carefully, just right.

Add some sugar, sweet and fine,

A pinch of salt, now it's time!

Sprinkle cinnamon, rich and bold,

Add ginger spice, the flavor of old.

Don't forget molasses goo,

It makes the dough stick just like glue!

Crack the eggs, then stir and blend,

Mix it well from end to end.

Little hands can roll the dough,

Into balls, watch the magic grow!

It's Time to Bake
Gingersnap Cookies

Roll each ball in sugar bright,

Sparkling like stars on a frosty night.

Place them gently on the tray,

The oven's ready, hip hooray!

The timer ticks, the minutes fly,

The scent of cookies fills the sky.

Oh, the smell, so warm and snug,

Like a toasty, gingery hug.

Ding, ding, ding! The cookies are done,

Golden brown, each and every one.

Let them cool, but don't you wait,

They're too yummy to hesitate!

Bite by bite, the crunch is clear,

A burst of spice brings lots of cheer.

Gingersnaps are the perfect snack,

It's Time to Bake
Gingersnap Cookies

With milk or tea, you'll want a stack!

Share with friends, share with all,

Big or little, short or tall.

Cookies made with care and heart,

Bring people together, that's the best part.

So, grab your apron, let's bake again,

Gingersnap cookies for family and friends.

Mix and roll, it's so much fun,

It's Time to Bake
Gingersnap Cookies

Baking's for everyone under the sun!

ABOUT THE CREATOR

Walter the Educator is one of the pseudonyms for Walter Anderson. Formally educated in Chemistry, Business, and Education, he is an educator, an author, a diverse entrepreneur, and he is the son of a disabled war veteran. "Walter the Educator" shares his time between educating and creating. He holds interests and owns several creative projects that entertain, enlighten, enhance, and educate, hoping to inspire and motivate you. Follow, find new works, and stay up to date with Walter the Educator™

at WaltertheEducator.com

www.ingramcontent.com/pod-product-compliance
Lightning Source LLC
LaVergne TN
LVHW052010060526
838201LV00059B/3946